STATES OF ETHIOPIA

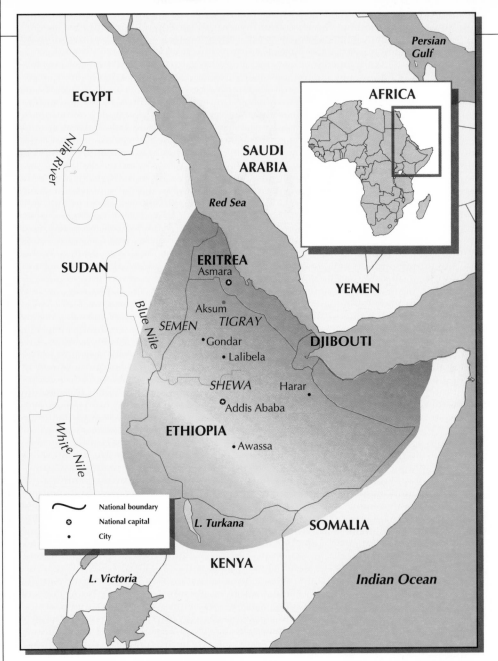

The territory of the states of Ethiopia extended beyond the borders of present-day Ethiopia.

~African Civilizations~

STATES OF ETHIOPIA

John Peffer
A First Book

Franklin Watts
A Division of Grolier Publishing
New York / London / Hong Kong / Sydney
Danbury, Connecticut

Photographs copyright ©: B. Seed/Viesti Associates, Inc.: pp. 8, 23, 49,
50, 56; Trip/Viesti Associates, Inc.: pp. 11, 13; H. Rogers/Viesti Associ-
ates, Inc.: pp. 15, 17, 45; Shaalini L.V. Ranasinghe: p. 20; J. Torregano/
Gamma Liaison: pp. 26, 35, 40; Wendy Stone/Gamma Liaison: p. 27;
Roger Wood/Corbis: p. 31; Jonathan Blair/Corbis: p. 38; The Newark
Museum/Art Resource, NY: p. 42; Hulton-Deutsch/Corbis: p. 53; John
Peffer: p. 54; Werner Forman Archive/Art Resource, NY: cover, p. 59.

Library of Congress Cataloging-in-Publication Data

Peffer, John.
    States of Ethiopia / John Peffer.
        p.   cm. — (African civilizations)
    Includes bibliographical references (p.) and index.
    Summary: Surveys the history and culture of the states of Ethiopia
in northeast Africa.
    ISBN 0-531-20278-X
    1. Ethiopia—History, Local—Juvenile literature. [1. Ethiopia—
History.]   I. Title.   II. Series.
DT381.P44   1998
963—dc21   97-37354
                                                            CIP
                                                            AC

CONTENTS

INTRODUCTION

Ethiopia is located in East Africa at the southern end of the Red Sea. For more than four thousand years peoples from Africa, Arabia, the Mediterranean, and Asia have mingled there. Ethiopia's long history has seen the rise and fall of several different states since ancient times. Unique forms of writing, literature, music, art, and architecture were developed in Ethiopia. Great cities were built at Aksum, Lalibela, Gondar, Harar, and Addis Ababa.

Thousands of years ago, the pharaohs of Egypt obtained incense in Ethiopia. In later centuries the wealth of Ethiopia came from its trade in exotic goods and slaves to countries throughout the Mediterranean Sea and the Indian Ocean.

One of the earliest states in Ethiopia was Aksum. The king of Aksum converted to Christianity around A.D. 330, and the Ethiopian Orthodox Church has been an important political force ever since. The outlying areas surrounding Aksum were called Ethiopia, a name that the ancient Greeks had originally used to describe all of Africa south of the Sahara Desert.

In the eighth century, the Christian state of Aksum lost control of its trade routes to Islamic states—states in which Islam was the official religion. Ethiopia's Christian center was forced to move south toward Lalibela. There, several centuries later, the Zagwe Dynasty recreated the glory of Aksum.

The Zagwe Dynasty was overthrown, in turn, by a dynasty from Amhara, a Christian dynasty that claimed descent from King Solomon of the Old Testament. For four hundred years these Solomonic kings were challenged by Islamic states to the east and south. The Christian kings of this period were nomadic warlords. They continually

Since A.D. 330, when the king of the Ethiopian state of Aksum converted to Christianity, most parts of what is now Ethiopia have been ruled by Christian emperors. The last emperor, Haile Selassie, was overthrown in 1974. He is seen here lighting a bonfire during Maskal, a celebration of the Ethiopian Orthodox Church.

moved their military camps and lived off the peasants in the territories they conquered. In the 1600s, however, a new Christian capital was built at Gondar. Painting, architecture, and literature flowered at the court. But Gondar declined because the rulers of various provinces within Ethiopia fought for control of the country.

The Christian Ethiopian state was reunited under Emperor Tewodros II in 1855, and the modern capital of Ethiopia was built at Addis Ababa by Emperor Menelik II in 1887. The last emperor of Christian Ethiopia, Haile Selassie, was overthrown in 1974.

BEGINNINGS OF ETHIOPIAN CIVILIZATION

Scholars believe that the earliest evidence of Ethiopia was provided by Queen Hatshepsut, an Egyptian pharaoh. Included in her burial temple, which was built near Thebes around 1500 B.C., are stone reliefs. The panels depict an expedition to a land that the ancient Egyptians called Punt, which was probably in the region of modern Ethiopia. The stone reliefs feature the inhabitants of Punt, including a queen or powerful woman, and the removal of myrrh trees to Egypt. Myrrh was used in ancient Egypt for incense, perfume, medicine, and spice.

The Saba people of South Arabia had great influence on the earliest known Ethiopian state, which was called D'MT. This stone tablet with engraved inscriptions was found in present-day Yemen, home of the ancient kingdom of Saba.

About five hundred years later, people from the kingdom of *Saba* in Arabia made the short journey across the Red Sea to Africa. They began settling among an Ethiopian farming people, the Agaw, who lived in northeastern Ethiopia. By 400 B.C. these two peoples had built urban centers and blended into a uniquely Ethiopian culture, which shared many similarities with the written language, religion, and stone architecture of South Arabia. Stone inscriptions from this early Ethiopian civilization, in a written language without vowels, tell of an Ethiopian state called D'MT (perhaps pronounced DAH-mot).

D'MT AND SABA

The relationship that existed between D'MT and the people from Saba is unclear. Perhaps the Sabaens in Ethiopia were refugees or colonists. D'MT towns were built in the area between the port of Adulis and the trade routes that led north to Egypt and Nubia and south to the interior of Ethiopia. This suggests that international trade was probably the key to the growth of the D'MT state.

Religious beliefs in D'MT and Saba were very similar. The ruins of D'MT temples and stone altars, once used to burn incense, resemble those in South Arabia. They are dedicated to some of the same deities, such as Astar, representing the planet Venus and fertility, and Ilmuqah, representing the moon and protection. Both D'MT and Saba incense altars often have discs and crescents carved on the front, probably symbols for Astar and possibly Mahrem, the god of war.

This Sabaen alabaster head might represent a deity that was worshiped in both Saba and D'MT. It originally had inlaid eyes and was attached to a larger sculpture.

Some experts believe that the rulers of D'MT combined the roles of priest and king. Statues of stiffly posed figures wearing robes, possibly representing deities or kings, have been found at such northern Ethiopian sites as Hawelti and Galamo.

For unknown reasons the D'MT state came to an end around 300 B.C. Traces of its civilization continued at Aksum, which rose to power in the same region two hundred years later.

2 THE RISE OF AKSUM

The earliest mention of Aksum is in the *Periplus of the Erythraean Sea*, a book about the navigation of the Red Sea, dating to around A.D. 50. This document mentions only that Zoskales was the king of Aksum, which was the name of both a state and its capital city.

Like D'MT before it, Aksum had a population that was a mix of Agaw and other Cushitic peoples with roots in South Arabia. Aksum grew and extended beyond the territory of D'MT. It had several large towns with smaller villages and farmlands in the outlying areas. As Aksum expanded it came to include a wide range of local peoples with

Stone architecture and the terracing of hillsides for farming are aspects of culture that the Sabaens introduced to Ethiopia. Above, a view of Yemen.

different religions, cultures, and languages. Plentiful water and rich soil around Aksum made it possible to feed a large population.

GOVERNMENT

Most of the population of Aksum were peasants who paid tribute, or taxes, to a local overlord. This meant that the rural overlords could demand food, labor, and military service from the local farmers. In turn, the overlords were obliged to send tribute to the king of Aksum.

This feudal system was easily extended when Aksum conquered other peoples, most of whom lived south of Aksum. Government of the new provinces was left in the hands of the local kings or rulers. They were obliged to send tribute to the king of Aksum, who was known as *Negus Negast*, meaning the king of kings, the ruler among equals.

The king of Aksum often strengthened the loyalty of local rulers by arranging for them to marry his relatives. Aksum's distant provinces often rebelled against the central power of Aksum, however, especially during those periods when the capital seemed weak. Sometimes they set up their own independent states.

TRADE

At first Aksum's wealth was probably based on farming, payment of tribute to the capital, and some local trade. As time passed, international trade, by both land and sea, became increasingly important. During the dry season, camel caravans traveled from Aksum along the dried-up beds of

One of Ethiopia's contributions to the world is the coffee bean, which was first grown there. The custom of drinking coffee quickly spread across the Red Sea from Ethiopia to Arabia, where these coffee pots were made.

the Takaze and Marab rivers into Nubia and Egypt. They also traveled to regions east and south for gold, ivory, animal pelts, slaves, and incense. The caravans carried these items to the coast to trade them for other goods from the Indian Ocean and the Mediterranean Sea.

Aksum's navy, based at Adulis, policed the ports along the Red Sea. The Persian religious leader, Manes, who founded the Manichean religion, wrote in the third century that Aksum was one of the four most important kingdoms in the world. The others were Persia, Rome, and China. At its height Aksum was a vital link in the trade between Africa and these other kingdoms.

HONORING KINGS AND GODS

From about A.D. 270 Aksum minted its own coins. The value of the coins was based on Roman currency, indicating the strong trade links between the two empires. Early Aksumite coins carried an image of the king with his name in Greek or in Ge'ez (pronounced GEEZ), a unique written language that was developed at Aksum. Along with Egyptian hieroglyphics and North African scripts, Ge'ez is one of the oldest known written languages in Africa. Ge'ez later evolved into the Amharic script, which is still used in Ethiopia today.

Early coins also featured the disc and crescent symbols. They are thought to represent Astar, the fertility god of D'MT, or Mahrem, the god of war who was the special deity and patron of the kings of early Aksum. The first kings of Aksum described themselves as sons of the "invincible god Mahrem." Kings were considered divine, and they may also have been priests. Little is known about the daily lives of the ordinary people of Aksum, but it is likely that they worshipped different gods than their kings did.

Mahrem was also honored in inscriptions on thrones and stone slabs that the kings of Aksum set up in conquered regions. The inscription on one throne, which once stood on the road between Aksum and Adulis but is now lost, was copied down by a Greek visitor in about 525. Known as the Adulis Inscription, it was probably written around 300. It describes an Aksumite king's military campaigns. His campaigns were conducted in various areas, from snow-covered regions to the desert. He attempted to unite different ethnic groups under his rule and "establish peace" so that trade—and tribute—could flow freely to him from throughout the land.

Aksum is famous for huge slabs carved from stone, called *stelae* (pronounced STEE-lee). Usually

The great stelae of Aksum were probably erected in memory of Aksumite kings.

found near royal tombs, stelae possibly commemorate deceased kings. Some are simply polished smooth. Others are carved like buildings extending into the heavens, complete with false doors and windows. Some of the Aksumite stelae reached 60 feet (18 m) in height. One stela, now fallen, rose to almost 100 feet (30 m).

The grand palaces of Aksum, built of rough stone and cement mixed from mud, had monumental staircases and waterspouts carved in the shapes of animal heads. These were the residences of the royalty and perhaps of the wealthy nobles, officials, and traders. Common people probably lived in round homes made of mud with thatched roofs.

THE CHRISTIAN ERA OF AKSUM

Around A.D. 330, the Roman emperor Constantine embraced Christianity and moved the capital of the empire from Rome east to Constantinople, present-day Istanbul, Turkey. At about the same time King Ezana of Aksum was converted to Christianity by his tutor, Frumentius of Tyre. Aksum became a Christian state, but the new faith was followed only by the elite, or the wealthy upper class.

Coins from this period display a cross; some of them carry the motto of Constantine, "By this sign you shall conquer." This suggests that the Christian God was now looked to for help in battle

Christianity became the state religion of Ethiopia at about the same time as it was declared legal in the Roman Empire by Constantine. Beautiful Ethiopian Orthodox crosses are one of many forms of Ethiopian Christian art.

instead of the Aksumite god Mahrem. Monuments commemorating great battles of that period refer to the "Lord of Heaven" instead of Mahrem. Later coins show the king wearing a pointed crown, similar to those worn in Europe, on one side of the coin. On the other side, the king wears a traditional Ethiopian head wrap.

FOREIGN TIES

Sharing the same religious faith as Constantinople strengthened Aksum's already close economic and political ties to the Roman Empire. Just as the Roman Empire was responsible for safe and free trade in the Mediterranean, Aksum protected the Red Sea.

Despite Ethiopia's ties to Constantinople, the Ethiopian Orthodox Church was more closely linked to the *Coptic* Christian Church of Egypt. The Egyptian church appointed a Coptic monk to serve as the patriarch, or religious head, of Ethiopia. The patriarch was called the *Abuna*. As a foreigner, the Abuna was often manipulated by the Ethiopian kings, who were ultimately the heads of the Ethiopian Orthodox Church.

The Orthodox Church of Ethiopia, the Coptic Church of Egypt, and some Syrian Christians followed a Christian doctrine called *Monophysitism*. The Church of the Roman Empire, which was the mother church, rejected this doctrine in A.D. 451. Aksum, following the lead of the Coptic Church of Egypt, held to its faith and split from the Church of the Roman Empire.

THE SPREAD OF CHRISTIANITY

Coptic missionaries fled persecution in the Roman Empire and came to Aksum to settle in the countryside. They began spreading the Christian faith to the rural people. The missionaries met with some resistance and persecution. The missionaries often built churches on sacred local sites, and the Aksumite army forced people to convert to Christianity.

During this period, impressive Christian monasteries, such as Debre Damo and Debre Libanos, were built on high, flat-topped mountains called *amba*. Over the centuries the monasteries often competed with one another for political power and control of the land. The leading monasteries were important centers of learning.

This Ethiopian painting represents the removal of the Ark of the Covenant from Jerusalem to Ethiopia, as described in the Ethiopian book *Kebre Negast*.

Certain traditions related to Christianity have been preserved only in Ethiopia, such as the biblical Book of Enoch. In addition, sacred dances, chants, and music played on trumpets, violins, and drums dating back to the age of ancient Aksum are still performed in Ethiopia. Some scholars believe that the Ark of the Covenant, containing the Ten Commandments given to Moses by God, is kept at Aksum in the Mary of Zion Cathedral.

THE DECLINE OF AKSUM

Aksum was at its height between the reigns of King Ezana, in about 330, and King Kaleb, who ruled until 543. Ezana is remembered for his con-

During Timqat festivities, clergy of the Ethiopian Orthodox Church carry replicas of the Ark of the Covenant on their heads.

version to Christianity as well as for his army's defeat of Meroë, a kingdom in the Nile valley. For hundreds of years after that, Aksum was the only major state in the region between the Nile and the Red Sea.

Early in the sixth century, Kaleb's army occupied the Jewish kingdom of Himyar in South Arabia. This was perhaps Aksum's last great territorial claim to the Arabian peninsula, where its army was defeated only a few years later.

By the end of the sixth century, Persians from the area known today as Iran began to dominate the Red Sea and the Eastern Mediterranean. Constantinople's fortunes declined, and Aksum suffered together with its close ally. In the seventh century Aksum's currency lost value, and Aksum eventually stopped minting coins. Although the city of Aksum remained the capital of the state, the nobility and the trading elite moved into the mountainous interior for safety.

Around 622, the followers of the Prophet Muhammad in Arabia, called Muslims, were being persecuted for their new religion, Islam. They were offered refuge in Aksum. As Islam spread, Muslim settlers occupied areas on the Ethiopian coast and the lowland plains to the southeast. The Dahlak Islands, just off the port of Adulis, were taken over by Muslims. These islands then became the international port instead of Adulis. Arab writers recorded that the new Muslim states on the coast continued to pay tribute to Ethiopia. They regarded Ethiopia as strong and called it by the name Abyssinia. After having been the dominant power in the Red Sea for more than two centuries, Aksum gradually declined in status to a minor trading nation.

According to legend, the Agaw people, who made up most of the population of the northern Ethiopian highlands, revolted against the weakened Aksumite state around 900. They were led by a queen named Gudit, who was opposed to the spread of Christianity and the Christian rulers of Ethiopia. Scholars do not know exactly what religion Gudit herself followed. Under Gudit, the Agaw destroyed the palaces and churches of the city of Aksum.

THE ZAGWE DYNASTY

Little is known about the century following the fall of Aksum. By the twelfth century a new line of kings called the Zagwe Dynasty had begun imitating the religion and government of Aksum. They built their new state in a mountainous region called Lasta, far from the ancient capital of Aksum.

THE ZAGWE PEOPLE

The Zagwe were descendants of Agaw people who had converted to Christianity and perhaps even married into the royal family of Aksum during its last days. They established a new political capital,

Lalibela—formerly called Roha—was named in honor of Emperor Lalibela, who is believed to have been responsible for the many rock-cut churches of Lalibela, such as the Church of St. Emanuel, above.

Adafa, and a nearby religious center called Roha. When they conquered new territories, they set up churches on the sacred sites of non-Christians. The Zagwe also built a chapel in Jerusalem for Ethiopian visitors.

The Zagwe were the first rulers of Ethiopia in a long time who had enough military and economic strength to force regional kings to submit to the authority of a single emperor. The Zagwe ruled the provinces of Wag, Lasta, Amhara, Tigray, and parts of Gondar and Gojjam. To the south, in Shewa, Muslims and native Sidamo peoples sent tribute to the Zagwe but remained outside the emperor's direct control.

The coastal part of Ethiopia directly on the Red Sea, known today as Eritrea, was ruled by Muslim states called *sultanates*. The coastal Muslims controlled the trade routes that connected East Africa to the Arab world, to India, and to the Mediterranean. The Zagwe controlled trade from the African interior and sent caravans to the Muslim-controlled coast.

EMPEROR LALIBELA

Emperor Lalibela (pronounced LUH-li-BEH-la), the brother of Zagwe King Harbe, reigned from 1185 to 1225. Roha was renamed Lalibela after him, and following his death he was declared a saint in the Ethiopian Orthodox Church.

Lalibela's life is the subject of many popular stories. One legendary account describes his visit to Egypt in 1209, where he went to request a new Abuna from the patriarch of the Coptic Church of Egypt. Crowds gathered to get a peek at Lalibela's fantastic procession through the streets of Cairo. The Christian Patriarch and the Islamic Sultan of Cairo were awed by the gifts that Lalibela presented them, including a gold crown, a giraffe, a lion, an elephant, and a zebra.

Another story describes an attempt to kill Lalibela. When Lalibela was younger and heir to the throne, plotters tried to poison him. Instead of killing him, however, the poison cured Lalibela of a tapeworm and put him to sleep for three days. While asleep Lalibela was taken to heaven by angels and shown the churches that he would later arrange to have carved in Roha. When he woke up he went to live as a hermit in the wilderness. From there he was again carried by angels, this time to Jerusalem.

Lalibela's mythic life story, which mirrors the story of the death and resurrection three days later of Jesus Christ, reinforced the Zagwe Dynasty's claim to be the heirs of the Kingdom of Israel and the rightful emperors of Christian Ethiopia.

THE CHURCHES OF LALIBELA

It is often said that Lalibela was responsible for the magnificent churches carved into the solid rock of the mountains of Lasta. In fact, similar churches were built in Lasta, Tigray, and Shewa before and after the reign of Lalibela.

Four of the twelve stone churches in Lasta were created by carving into the underlying rock, starting at ground level. This soft red rock, called *tufa*, is relatively easy to carve at first, but hardens once it has been exposed to air for some time.

First a pit was cut into the surface of the earth outlining a rectangular section of rock. The top layers of the churches were created when the surrounding pit was shallow; the lower levels were carved as the pit was deepened.

At every stage workmen carved into the rock to form windows and then halls within. The exterior surfaces were made to look exactly like a building made from bricks of stone, complete with brick-like texture, pillars, doors, and windows. The final

A hermit in a church in Lalibela meditates on the First and Second Books of Kings, the books of the Old Testament most sacred to Ethiopians.

result was a freestanding church carved of solid rock.

Other carved churches associated with Lalibela were cut into the faces of cliffs or excavated underground with connecting tunnels. According to one of the Lalibela stories, angels helped build the churches by continuing the work at night, when the stonemasons were asleep.

The Lalibela churches imitate the architecture of Aksum. The entire complex of buildings was meant to evoke the city of Jerusalem. A stream running though the area was named after the Jordan River in Israel. Lalibela's goal was to imitate the glory of Aksum and to create a New Jerusalem to unify his people.

5 THE SOLOMONIC DYNASTY

Yekuno Amlak, an ambitious prince of Amhara province in the late thirteenth century, set out to become the emperor of Christian Ethiopia. He diverted trade in his southern region, Shewa, away from Lasta, which made the Amhara rich. He promised independence and land to church leaders throughout Ethiopia in return for their support. In particular, he gained the support of the monk Tekele Haymanot, who led the powerful monastery of Debre Damo.

Around 1270 Yekuno Amlak incited a rebellion in the southern province of Shewa and killed Naakute Laab, the last Zagwe emperor, in battle.

An aerial view of the monastery of Debre Damo.

The heir of the Zagwe Dynasty had the support of the Debre Libanos monastery in Tigray. He unsuccessfully fought to reclaim the empire.

After Yekuno Amlak was victorious, Tekele Haymanot's monastery was rewarded with a huge land grant. The area comprised one third of the land of the new Ethiopian state, which the Ethiopian Orthodox Church controlled for hundreds of years. Tekele Haymanot later founded the monastery of Debre Asbo in Shewa, an important center of worship and education. After his death he was made a saint in the Ethiopian Orthodox Church. Religious paintings show Tekele Haymanot standing on one leg, a miraculous feat of stamina he supposedly performed for years on end, until eventually his unused leg withered and fell off.

The Ethiopian state immediately became dominated by the language and culture of the Amhara, who were a minority. Supported by important church leaders, the Amharic authorities destroyed the records of the Zagwe and accused them of being false heirs to the royal line of Aksum. To be of royal blood now meant being either from Amhara or from Tigray, which was the site of ancient Aksum.

THE MYTH OF THE SOLOMONIC DYNASTY

The Amharic rulers used an ancient myth to justify their rule: the legend of the Queen of Sheba. It was written down by Tigrayan scribes during the early fourteenth century in a book called the *Kebre Negast*, which means the glory of kings.

The story states that the Queen of Sheba, who

This Ethiopian painting represents the meeting of Makeda and Solomon described in *Kebre Negast*.

is mentioned in the biblical book First Book of Kings, was named Makeda and was a Queen of Aksum. According to the myth, Makeda traveled to Jerusalem to learn about governing from the wise King Solomon. Solomon tricked her into sleeping with him, and she later bore his son. The son was educated by Solomon and then returned to Ethiopia after stealing the Ark of the Covenant. According to the *Kebre Negast*, the son of Makeda and Solomon was Menelik I, first king of Aksum and ancestor of Yekuno Amlak.

With this story the Amharic rulers of Christian Ethiopia claimed to be God's Chosen People and descendants of the tribe of Israel. Yekuno Amlak's lineage was called the Solomonic Dynasty, and they ruled Ethiopia for four hundred years.

THE EMPEROR

Under the Solomonic Dynasty, the emperor, or Negus Negast, was hidden from public view behind a curtain. He was considered semi-divine, and visitors were required to lie on the ground before him. Despite the national myth of the Solomonic Dynasty, emperors were not always direct descendants of past rulers. Each emperor chose his own successor with the help of advisers at his court. Until the nineteenth century the Negus Negast had many wives and, therefore, many potential heirs to the throne. Traditionally, the emperor's heirs were kept imprisoned at a monastery or some distant part of the country. They were held so they could not attempt to take the throne before their time.

EUROPE AND THE RISE OF ISLAM

During the early years of the Solomonic Dynasty, craftspeople and artists from medieval Europe

The art of the Ethiopian Orthodox Church during the Solomonic Dynasty, such as this icon of the Madonna and Child, is similar in style to that used widely in Eastern Europe and used formerly in Constantinople.

worked in Ethiopia and influenced local styles of architecture and religious painting. Much Ethiopian art from this period looks like the Christian art of Eastern Europe, which had been influenced centuries before by Constantinople.

In 1424 Emperor Yeshak I wrote a letter to the king of Spain requesting skilled artisans. A few

Italian adventurers and artists from Florence and Venice also came to work for Ethiopian emperors during the fifteenth century, and Ethiopian priests and pilgrims visited the Vatican in Rome.

The rise of Islamic states along the eastern Mediterranean Sea and the Red Sea, however, hampered the frequent communication between Christian Europe and Ethiopia that had existed in the past. Still, Ethiopia was not forgotten in Europe. A popular European story claimed that a mythical king, called *Prester John*, ruled a Christian kingdom in the faraway land of Ethiopia. It was believed that Prester John might someday help Europe conquer the lands and trade routes dominated by Muslims.

In fact, for many centuries Christian Ethiopia was itself concerned with curbing the growing Islamic influence within Ethiopia and in neighboring states.

6 ISLAMIC STATES AND GONDAR

In the early years of the Solomonic Dynasty, Muslim *sultanates* were established on the Ethiopian coast and in the hot, low-lying regions of eastern Ethiopia, in Shewa, Ifat, Adal, and Harar. Muslims intermarried with local people, including the Somali nomads and the Sidamo people of Shewa.

In times of peace these Islamic sultanates played an important role in international trade, but they also competed with Christian Ethiopia for commercial and religious influence. The sultans of the Walasma Dynasty in Ifat, for example, controlled the caravan route from the coast to the highlands after 1285.

Islamic coins from various periods

RELIGIOUS CONFLICTS

Communities of Muslims, called *jabarti*, lived within Christian territories, but they were discriminated against for many centuries. Although the *jabarti* provided valuable services as lawyers, merchants, craftspeople, and healers in the Christian kingdom, they were not allowed to farm or own land. Even in the seventeenth century, *jabarti* in the Christian capital could not live near, marry, or associate with Christians outside of business transactions. As late as 1878, Emperor Yohannes IV tried unsuccessfully to convert all Muslims to Christianity.

A major source of conflict was the Christian state's demand that the sultanates pay them taxes. Emperor Amada Seyon in the early fourteenth century and Emperor Zara Yakob in the fifteenth century are remembered for defeating the Muslim states of Ifat and Harar in battle and forcing them to pay taxes.

In 1527 the Muslims of Adal revolted when the Christian army came to collect taxes. The revolt was led by the military commander Ahmad ibn-Ibrahim, also called Gragn, the left-handed. He believed that the Muslim faith had weakened in the wealthy capitals of Harar and Ifat. He declared and led a *jihad,* or Islamic holy war, to enforce what he considered a purer form of Islam. Ahmad ibn-Ibrahim took his jihad to the highlands, conquered the Christian territories, and destroyed the ancient cathedral known as Mary of Zion at Aksum.

The Christian emperor, Gelawdewos, sent word of his plight to the Portuguese, who sent four hundred soldiers armed with muskets to Ethiopia. After terrible losses on both sides and the death in battle of Gelawdewos, Ahmad ibn-Ibrahim and his Turkish allies were defeated in 1543 near Lake Tana. Despite being pushed out of the Christian kingdom, the Muslim armies of Harar continued to threaten the kingdom until about 1577.

Gelawdewos's successor, Emperor Susneyos, was eager for further aid from Europe. Roman Catholic missionaries, who had accompanied the Portuguese soldiers to Ethiopia, were allowed to remain in Ethiopia as a sign of the emperor's appreciation. He unwisely declared Roman Catholicism to be the state religion in 1614. This outraged the leaders of the Ethiopian Orthodox Church and many of their peasant followers.

Susneyos also tried to make the kingdom more democratic. Under Susneyos's rule, Agaw and Oromo peoples were given influential positions at court. Although they made up the majority, they had been considered inferior to the ruling Tigray and Amhara. In addition, Susneyos refused to remain hidden from his people the way past emperors had done, and his visitors were no longer required to lie down before him. Susneyos became very unpopular among conservative princes, who did not want the power of the ruling class lessened.

Dissatisfaction with Susneyos caused a minor civil war. Realizing his unpopularity, Susneyos stepped down and gave the throne to his son Fasiledes in 1632.

EMPEROR FASILEDES AND GONDAR

Fasiledes took a course opposite to his father's. To Fasiledes, Europeans seemed a bigger threat to national unity than Islam. He banned the Portuguese and all Roman Catholics from the country. He negotiated treaties with the Islamic rulers of Turkey and Arabia to keep Europeans away from the ports of Ethiopia and to allow free passage to Muslim traders. Diplomatic relations with Portugal were not resumed for three hundred years.

Until the seventeenth century the Solomonic Dynasty had no stable source of income. Emperors moved from village to village demanding support from the people, putting down rebellions and enlarging the empire as they went. Their courts were huge military camps that crossed the countryside in search of fuel and food, disrupting the local people wherever they moved.

Fasiledes established a royal capital near Lake

An overview of Gondar

Tana at Gondar, which remained the capital for the next two hundred years. At its height, almost 100,000 people lived there.

The arts flourished at Gondar. Richly decorated palaces, churches, and a royal bath were

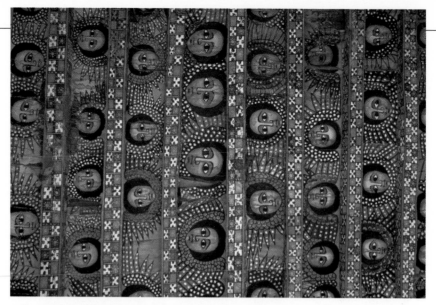

Ceiling painting in Debre Berhan Selassie Church in Gondar

built with the help of Muslim and Jewish crafts-people. Schools of biblical study, dance, poetry, and painting were established. Painted manuscripts and portable *icons*, religious images that depict holy persons and events, took on a more local character. Images of the Virgin Mary and the infant Jesus were given African features and dress. Also popular were Christian saints known only in Ethiopia, such as Saint Tekele Haymanot and Saint Qeddus, who lived the life of a hermit, befriended wild animals, and was covered with hair by God to hide his nakedness.

Gondar declined during the eighteenth century as the emperors lost control over the provinces, although they remained the symbolic leaders of the state. Each head, or *ras,* of the local provinces fought the others for power. This period is called *Zamana Mesafint,* the Era of Judges. It is named after a biblical period when a ruler was like a puppet, controlled by lesser, regional leaders.

THE ERA OF JUDGES

During the Era of Judges (1769–1855), Shewa, Tigray, Semen, Lasta, and the Muslim sultanates acted as separate kingdoms. For one hundred years the common people found little protection from their own rulers as civil war raged and soldiers attacked villages for food.

The emperors during this period were members of an Oromo family from Yejju. This family had converted to Islam, married into the Gondar royal family, and then converted to Christianity in order to rule the Ethiopian state.

This capture of the royal house was a significant achievement for the Oromo. They were a cattle-herding people who had begun moving into the center of Ethiopia from the south of the country during the jihad of Ahmad ibn-Ibrahim in the sixteenth century. By the eighteenth century the Oromo outnumbered most other groups in the empire. They adopted the customs, farming methods, and languages of the local people, becoming Muslim in some areas, Christian in others.

In some areas the Oromo retained their traditional form of government, an age-based system called *gada*, alongside new religious and political customs. *Gada* placed authority in the hands of men over age forty.

THE NEW SOLOMONIC DYNASTY

The Era of Judges ended in 1855, when Emperor Tewodros II brought the warring provincial rulers under control and forced the Oromo rulers of Gondar back to the province of Yejju. He began a new Solomonic Dynasty.

His successors, Yohannes IV and then Menelik II, modernized Ethiopia. Menelik II founded a new provincial capital in Shewa, named Addis Ababa, which means "new flower" in Amharic. It became the national capital in 1889, when Menelik II also granted Italy control of the northern province of Eritrea.

Nineteenth-century Ethiopian soldiers

A contemporary painting of the Battle of Adowa, during which the Ethiopians defeated the Italians

The Italian government later claimed that this document gave them control of all Ethiopia. When the Italians invaded Ethiopia in 1896, they were defeated at the Battle of Adowa. Thereafter, European nations recognized the independence of Ethiopia.

7
ETHIOPIA IN MODERN TIMES

In the last century Ethiopia has played an important role in international politics. The history of Ethiopia, both ancient and modern, has been a symbol of pride and unity for people of African descent worldwide.

In 1916 Ras Teferi Mekonnen was named heir to the Ethiopian throne and regent to Menelik's daughter, Empress Zewditu. A capable diplomat, in 1928 Ras Teferi brought Ethiopia into the League of Nations, which later became the United Nations. In 1930 Zewditu died, and Ras Teferi was crowned Emperor Haile Selassie.

The Rastafarian movement was named after Ras Teferi, crowned Emperor Haile Selassie. A lion beside a guard outside the former palace is a reminder of the title "Lion of Judah," one of the titles of Ethiopian emperors, from Menelik I through Haile Selassie.

Shortly after Ras Teferi was crowned emperor, a new movement started in Jamaica. Followers of Marcus Garvey, an influential black nationalist born in Jamaica, believed that Haile Selassie was the Messiah and a symbol of a new era in the struggles of black people everywhere. Emperor Haile Selassie did not see himself this way. Nonetheless, this was the beginning of the Rastafarian religious movement, which has had a great influence on Western music and youth culture since the 1960s.

In 1935, Italy again invaded Ethiopia. The Italian occupation outraged many blacks in Africa and the United States, further urging many to fight against Italy and Germany during World War II. Ethiopia was liberated from the Italians in 1941. After World War II Ethiopia's proud independence inspired other African nations to overthrow European colonialism.

Emperor Haile Selassie opened public schools and a university, built hospitals and modern cities, and put an end to slavery. But his reforms were not enough for the many Ethiopians who continued to struggle in poverty on lands owned by the royalty and the Ethiopian Orthodox Church. When a terrible famine devastated much of North Africa in the 1970s, Ethiopian military leaders took advantage of popular discontent and overthrew Haile Selassie in 1974. He died in prison a year later. He was the last emperor of Ethiopia.

ETHIOPIA AFTER THE EMPERORS

The new Ethiopian military government, which was strongly backed by the former Soviet Union, gave lands owned by the royalty and the church to the peasants. But it also forced other peasants off their own lands. This created a food shortage that turned deadly when another drought struck in the early 1980s. Civil war broke out in several regions where the government was unpopular. When the Soviet Union collapsed in 1991, the unpopular Ethiopian government fell too. In 1993, Eritrea, which was formerly part of Ethiopia, declared itself an independent nation. The Oromo people also desire to be independent from Ethiopia.

Apart from the brief Italian occupation, Ethiopia is the only African country that was never colonized by Europe. Its proud past and generous

Fragment of a ceremonial fan depicting Ethiopian Orthodox saints

resources hold out great promise for the twenty-first century. Although the Ethiopian Orthodox Church no longer holds the same power it once did, it is one of the oldest Christian churches in the world. Its monuments recall the past glories of the ancient states of Ethiopia.

TIMELINE

1500 B.C.	Stone reliefs of Punt carved for Hatshepsut's burial temple
500 B.C.	Rise of kingdom of Saba and Ethiopian state of D'MT
A.D. 50	King Zoskales of Aksum in *Periplus of the Erythraean Sea*
330	King Ezana of Aksum converts to Christianity
525	King Kaleb conquers kingdom of Himyar in South Arabia
700	Muslim sultanates develop on Red Sea coast and in southern Ethiopia
900	Gudit and the Agaw destroy the city of Aksum
1100	Zagwe Dynasty builds capital at Adafa, Lalibela churches
1270	Rise of Amharic Solomonic Dynasty
1280–1500s	Rise of Ifat and other Muslim sultanates
1531	Muslim army conquers the Christian state
1543	Gelawdewos and Portuguese defeat Muslim army
1632	Susneyos abdicates in favor of his son, Fasiledes
1630s	Fasiledes builds capital at Gondar; Portuguese and Roman Catholics banned; artistic renaissance
1769–1855	Yejju Oromo capture the royal throne; Era of Judges
1855	Tewodros II reunites Christian empire of Ethiopia
1930	Haile Selassie crowned emperor
1935	Italian invasion
1941	Ethiopia liberated from the Italian occupation
1974	Haile Selassie dethroned by military coup

GLOSSARY

Abuna patriarch of the Ethiopian Orthodox Church

Coptic concerning the Christian church that originated in Egypt and that follows Monophysitism

gada age-based system of government of the Oromo

icon religious image depicting a holy person or event that is used for devotional purposes

jabarti Muslims who lived among Christian Ethiopians

jihad Islamic holy war

Kebre Negast Glory of kings; book about the origin of the Solomonic Dynasty

Monophysitism doctrine about Jesus Christ followed by the Ethiopian Orthodox Church

Negus Negast King of Kings; title of Ethiopian emperor

Prester John in medieval Europe, mythical ruler of a Christian kingdom in Africa

ras head; title of provincial leaders in Christian Ethiopia

Saba ancient kingdom based in South Arabia that influenced Ethiopian culture

stelae slabs or pillars of carved stone used for commemorative purposes

sultanate a Muslim state

tufa soft red rock from which several Ethiopian churches were carved

Zamana Mesafint Era of Judges; period when *ras*es had more power than Ethiopian emperor

FOR FURTHER READING

Fradin, Dennis B. *Ethiopia*. Chicago: Children's Press, 1988.

Kurz, Jane. *Ethiopia: The Roof of Africa*. New York: Dillon, 1991.

Mann, Kenny. *Egypt, Kush, Aksum: Northeast Africa*. New York: Dillon, 1997.

FOR ADVANCED READERS

Gerster, Georg. *Churches in Rock: Early Christian Art in Ethiopia*. New York: Phaidon, 1970.

Heldman, M., ed. *African Zion: The Sacred Art of Ethiopia*. New Haven, CT: Yale University Press, 1993.

Pankhurst, Richard, and Denis Gerard. *Ethiopia Photographed: Historic Photographs of the Country and Its People*. New York: Columbia University Press, 1996.

WEB SITES

Due to the changeable nature of the Internet, sites may appear and disappear very quickly. Internet addresses must be entered with capital and lowercase letters exactly as they appear.

Ethiopia Page: http://www.cs.indiana.edu/hyplan/dmulholl/ethiopia/ethiopia.html

Ethiopian Jewry Homepage: http://www.cais.com/nacoej

Ethiopian Related News and Info: http://www.ethio.com

INDEX

ABOUT THE AUTHOR

John Peffer received a bachelor's degree in African Studies from the Individualized Major Program at Indiana University and a master's degree in Art History from Columbia University. He has conducted research in South Africa on a Fulbright grant and is currently writing a doctoral dissertation on art schools in South African townships.